GOD
is in the
DETAILS!

VOLUME 1

FINDING
JOY
IN THE
LITTLE THINGS

GOD IS IN THE DETAILS

Trade Paperback ISBN 9780692981634

Cover design by Harvest Creek Design; cover image by Teresa Granberry
Illustrated by Teresa Granberry; devotions by Samuel Granberry

Published in the United States.

This book is available at special quantity discount when purchased in bulk by corporations, organizations, or special-interest groups.   For more information, please contact teresa@harvestcreek.net.

SEEK GOD IN THESE SIMPLE DESIGNS

Drawing and doodling have been an integral part of my life. As a young student, I would scribble designs on my paper while listening to the teacher, not realizing there was a brain-to-hand connection involved in my learning style. Even now, I use that same process when taking notes in a corporate meeting or during a church sermon.

We were made in the image of the Master Designer, the God of all creation. And a small spark of creativity has been planted in each of us, as a reflection of His glory. The same God - who knew to bless us through green grass and a blue sky - is the One who speaks to us through Art and Design.

The word "design" means to set apart for a certain purpose. Each design in this book was developed with a particular thought or scripture to focus on while coloring. As you creatively fill in the drawing or jot down your reflections, allow your mind to be filled with God's truth.

You won't find angry or filthy words in these designs. That's not healthy for your soul and it only breeds more frustration. These verses were chosen to build you up and be a respite from the cares of life.

My prayer is that the Lord will inspire you, encourage you, and fill your heart with a renewed attitude as you color in each detail within these pages. Remember, He can be found in the little things!

Teresa Granberry
Harvest Creek Design

TIPS & TRICKS FOR SUCCESS:

Place a clean sheet of paper under the page while coloring. This will prevent colors from bleeding through to the next page.

You don't have to start with the first page! Scroll through the book and begin at a place that grabs your attention.

Use patterns, as well as colors to fill in the designs. A series of lines, dots, plaids or curly-q's will add individual personality to your artwork.

ALL
NATURE
Sings

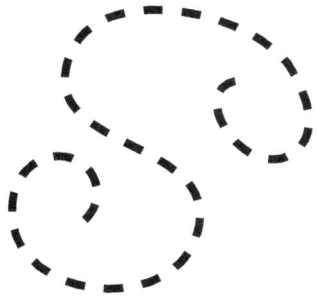

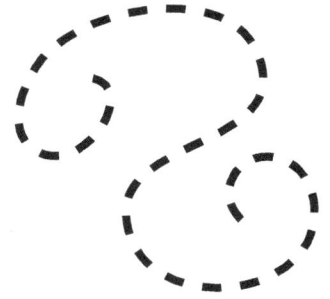

Many of us tend to be starters, but not finishers. We are inflicted with the dreaded "start-it-itis" disease. That is, we begin a project then quickly lack interest and move on to another. Our God is both a starter and a finisher.   He began a good work in you, and will see it through to completion.

He never loses interest in us, nor turns away from the plan chosen for us at the time of our conception.   The Lord continues to refine us until we have come to the end of our journey.

What gives you confidence that the Lord is working in your life and is faithful to completion?

I am confident of this one thing.

He will complete His good work in me.

The Biblical definition for a home encompasses one's entire family. It refers to more than a domestic building or dwelling place, but rather to an entire line of descendants.

The Hebrew word for house [bayith or beth] often translates to armory and means "to cover". When one makes a decree that they and their house will serve the Lord, the proclamation includes every person in their family lineage.

As you color this page, reflect on God's promises which cover current and future members of your family.

Bless the Lord for His protective covering over your home and over the future of your family.

His love extends to a thousand generations of those who love Him and keep His commandments. Ex. 20:6

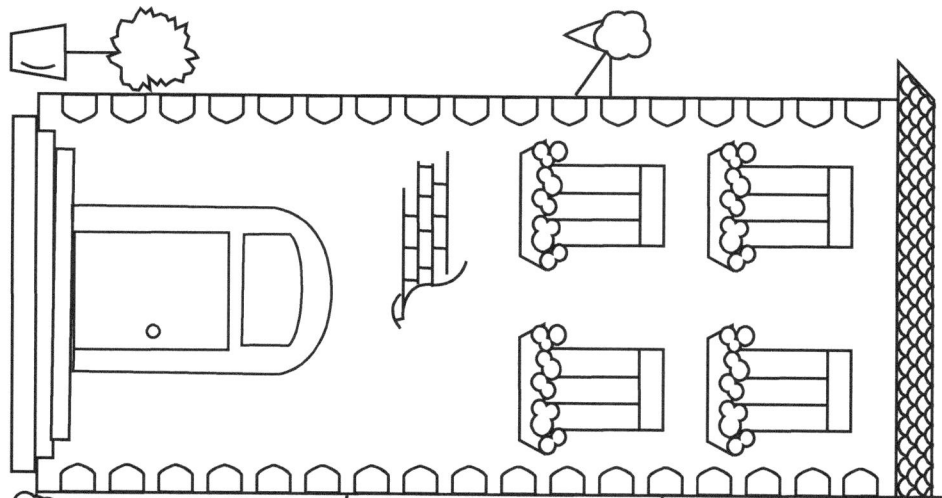
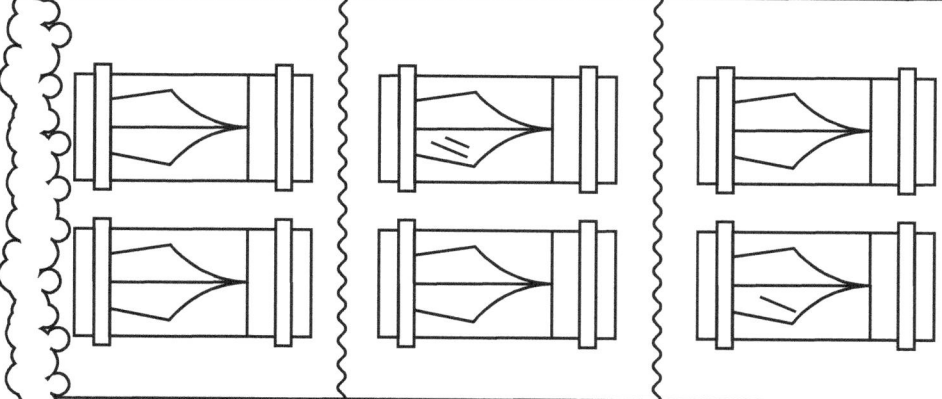
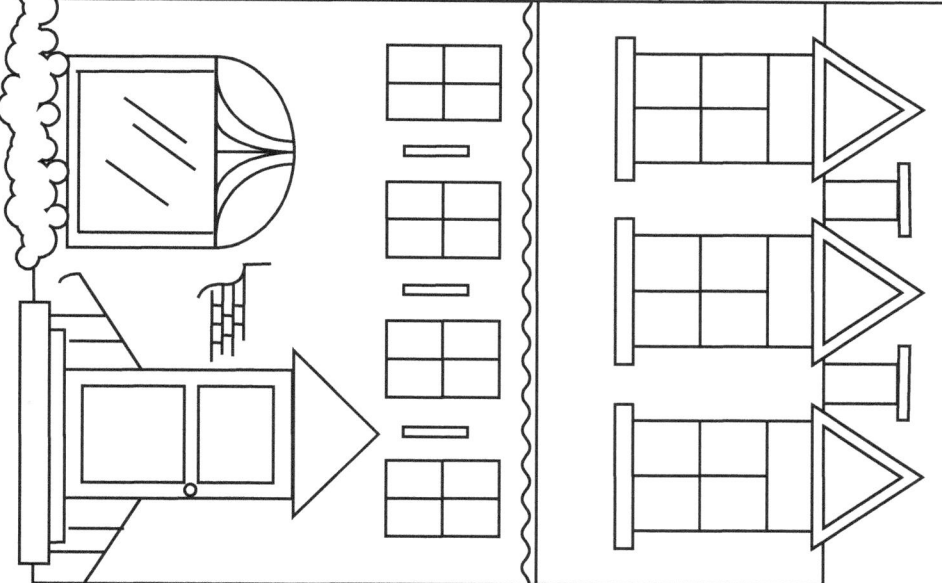
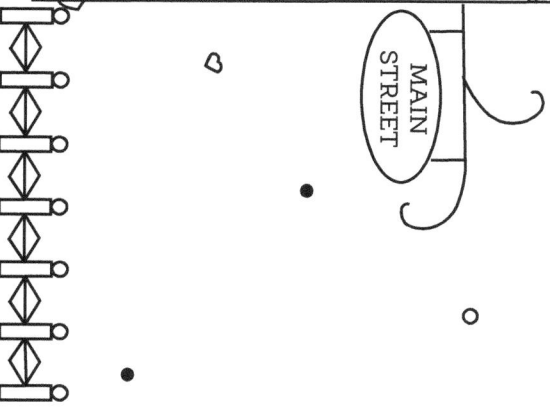

As for me and my house, we will serve the Lord.

MAIN STREET

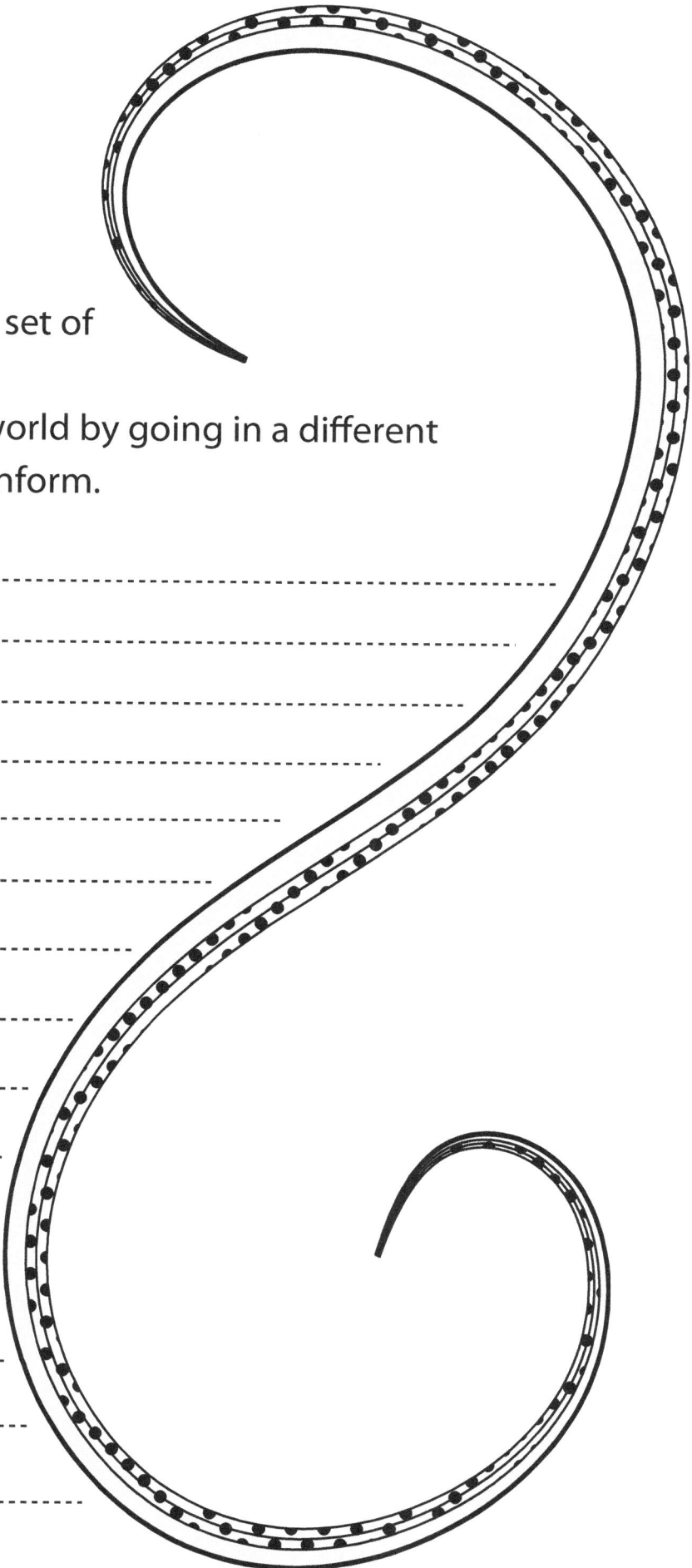

As Christians, we need a different set of standards to live by.

List ways you can transform the world by going in a different direction than with those who conform.

Do not conform to the pattern of this world,
but be transformed by the renewing of your mind.

The Lord is always with me. I will not be shaken!

Has Life ever taken you by surprise?

Perhaps something happened that was completely out of your control (or at least it seemed that way).

God doesn't change because something happens that we weren't expecting.

Nothing is out of His sight.

List below the cares that you will cast on Him.

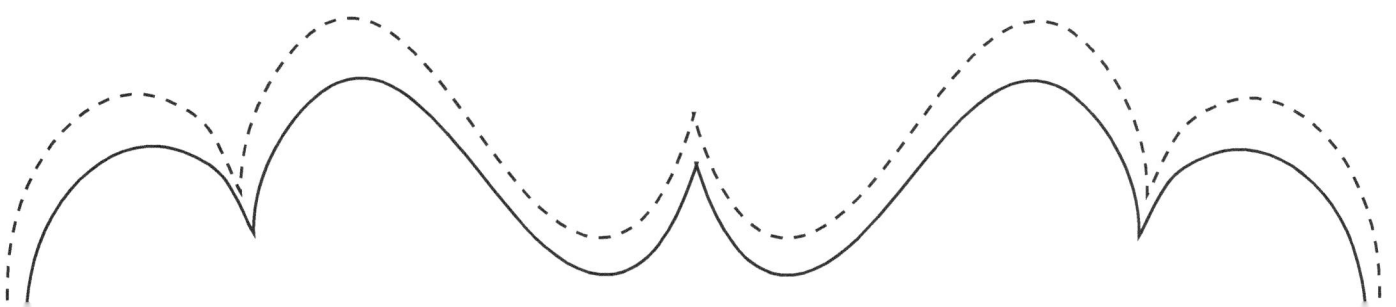

Don't PANIC. I'm with you. There's **NO NEED TO FEAR**, for I am your God.

Drawing Close to someone means to

move toward them in a comfortable position. It causes you to intimately connect with them in a way that can make you feel vulnerable, yet blessed.

It is hard to achieve true intimacy with God because we don't fully understand what that entails. We must give Him our secrets, our passions, our desires, and trust that He will accept them without judgment. That often makes us uncomfortable.

God wants you to make the first move. Draw near to Him without fear or reservation.

Rest assured, He yearns to be with you.

Draw close to God, and God will draw close to you.

James 4:8

Absolutely Everything

ALL OF IT

Visible & Invisible

EVERYTHING

Above & Below

FOR ABSOLUTELY
EVERYTHING,
ABOVE
AND BELOW,
VISIBLE
AND INVISBLE,

GOT STARTED
IN HIM
AND
FINDS ITS
PURPOSE
IN HIM.

TODAY
be confident
in God's plan
for you.
Have a
GREAT
DAY

FOR

I KNOW

THE PLANS

I HAVE

FOR

YOU

AND I WILL
GIVE YOU
A NEW
HEART,
AND A NEW
SPIRIT
I WILL PUT
WITHIN YOU.

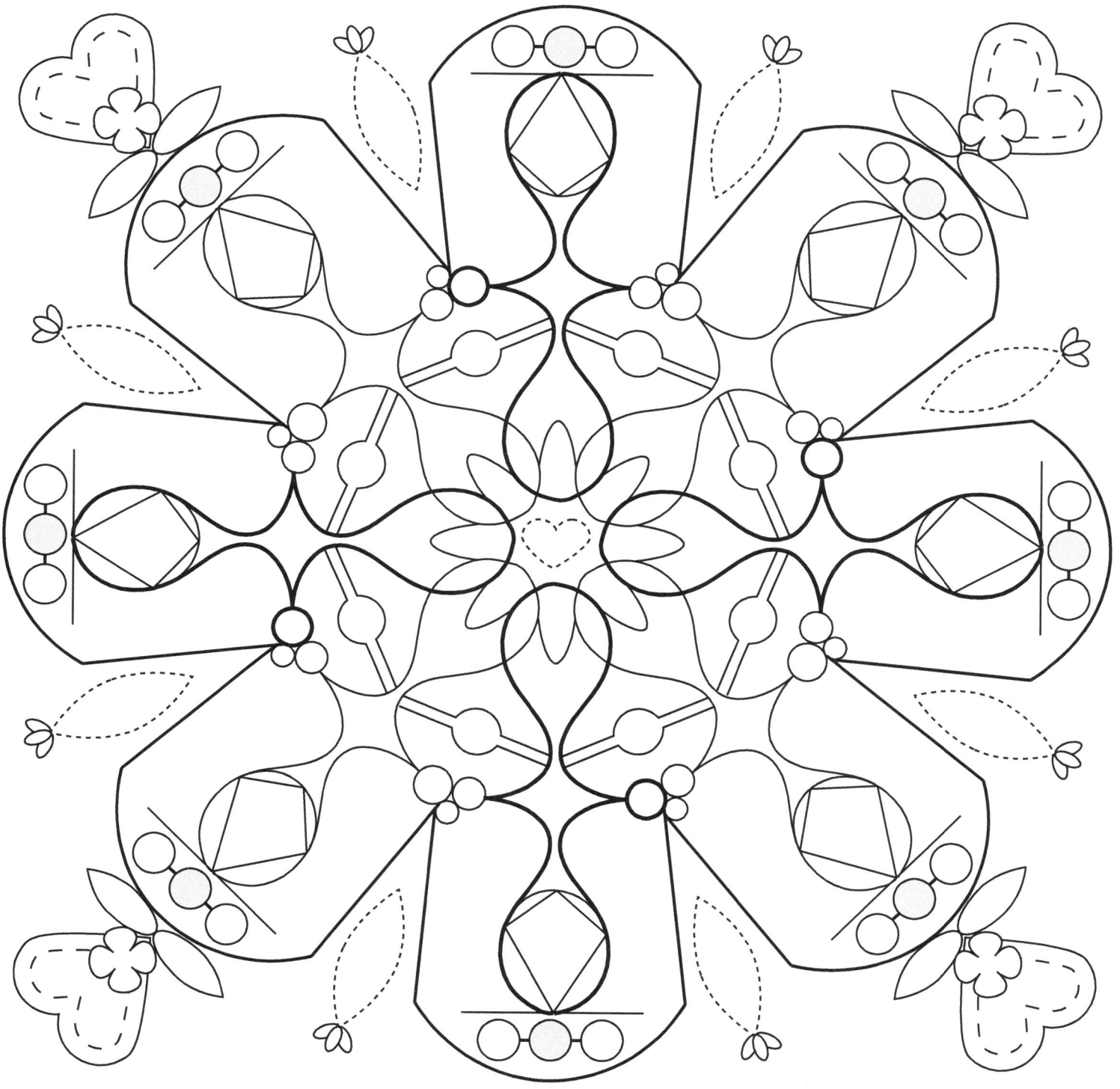

AM I BEARING FRUIT?

....

....

....

....

....

....

....

....

....

....

Herein is my **FATHER** *glorified that ye bear much fruit.* John 15:8

GOD HAS PLANTED YOU LIKE STRONG AND GRACEFUL OAKS FOR HIS OWN GLORY

Details, details, details.

It's been said that, "Details create the BIG picture."

Even major projects are dependent on the smallest components.

One may ask, "Does God care about the details of my life?"

The answer is Yes!

Your heavenly Father knows every single hair on your head.

And as a loving parent, He knows what's best for you.

Every decision we make becomes a small component in the big picture
of our life. There is significance in everything we do.
Therefore, we should seek the Father's guidance in every step.

Thank the Lord for His concern regarding
the details of your life. Thank Him for weaving the fabric of every
decision you make into a beautiful quilt - that is,
your very existence.

Are not two sparrows sold for a penny? Yet not one of them will fall to the
ground outside your Father's care. And even the very hairs
of your head are all numbered. So don't be afraid;
you are worth more than many sparrows. Matt. 10:29-31

God enjoys
every detail
of your Life!

TODAY
I am Shankful for:

* ✽ ....
* ✽ ....
* ✽ ....
* ✽ ....
* ✽ ....
* ✽ ....
* ✽ ....

This is the day the Lord has made.

I will rejoice and be glad in it.

WAYS GOD SHOWS LOVE TO ME

GOD is LOVE

GOD is LOVE

The Bible says that we are in this world, but not of this world. Sometimes we need to remind ourselves that this is only a temporary stopover.   We are on our way to a place that is unimaginably wonderful - the kingdom of God.

Take a moment and list some of the things that will be different in the life that is to come:

Jesus said, "My kingdom is not of this world...
My kingdom is from another place."
John 18:36

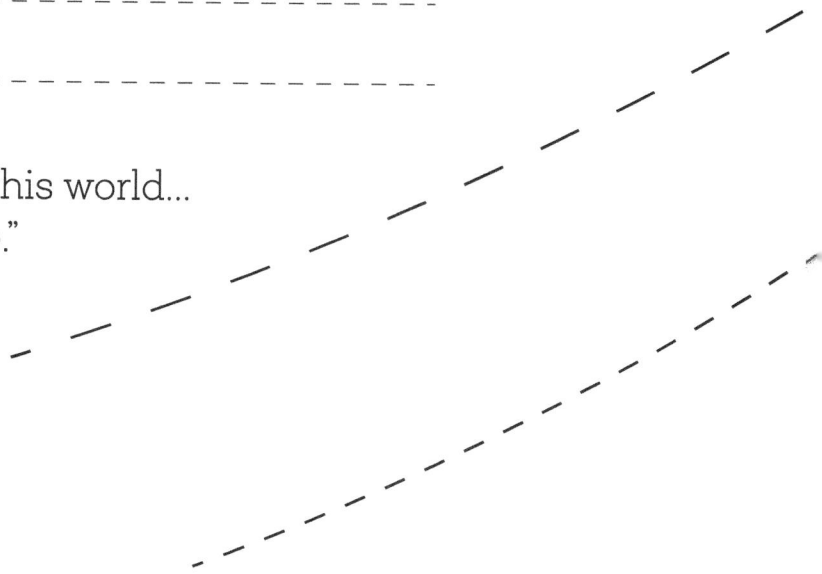

This life is preparation for the next!

TIMES CHANGE

PEOPLE CHANGE

JOBS CHANGE

GOVERNMENTS CHANGE

FRIENDS CHANGE

PROBLEMS CHANGE

But

GOD NEVER CHANGES

WHAT DOES A mature CHRISTIAN

LOOK LIKE?

GOD WANTS US TO GROW UP,
LIKE CHRIST IN EVERYTHING.

God is a caring father.

His love is often incomprehensible.

He cares about us more than we care about ourselves.

There are times when we may not feel His presence
or understand that He's really close at hand.

But that doesn't change the fact that He
will never leave us or forsake us.

We have a good, good Father.

Reflect on the ways He has demonstrated His care for you.

God CARES ABOUT ME

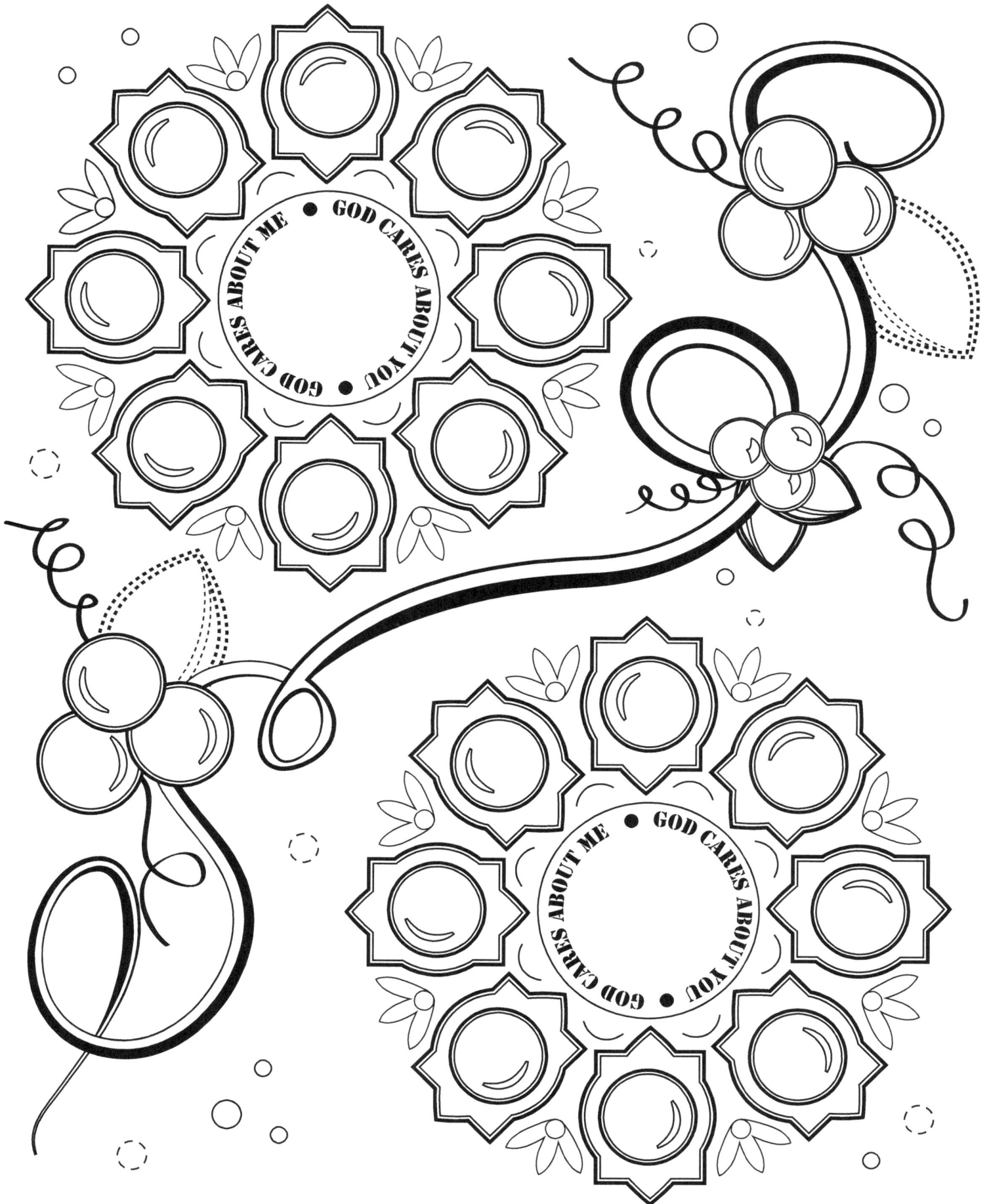

GOD CARES ABOUT ME • GOD CARES ABOUT YOU

GOD CARES ABOUT ME • GOD CARES ABOUT YOU

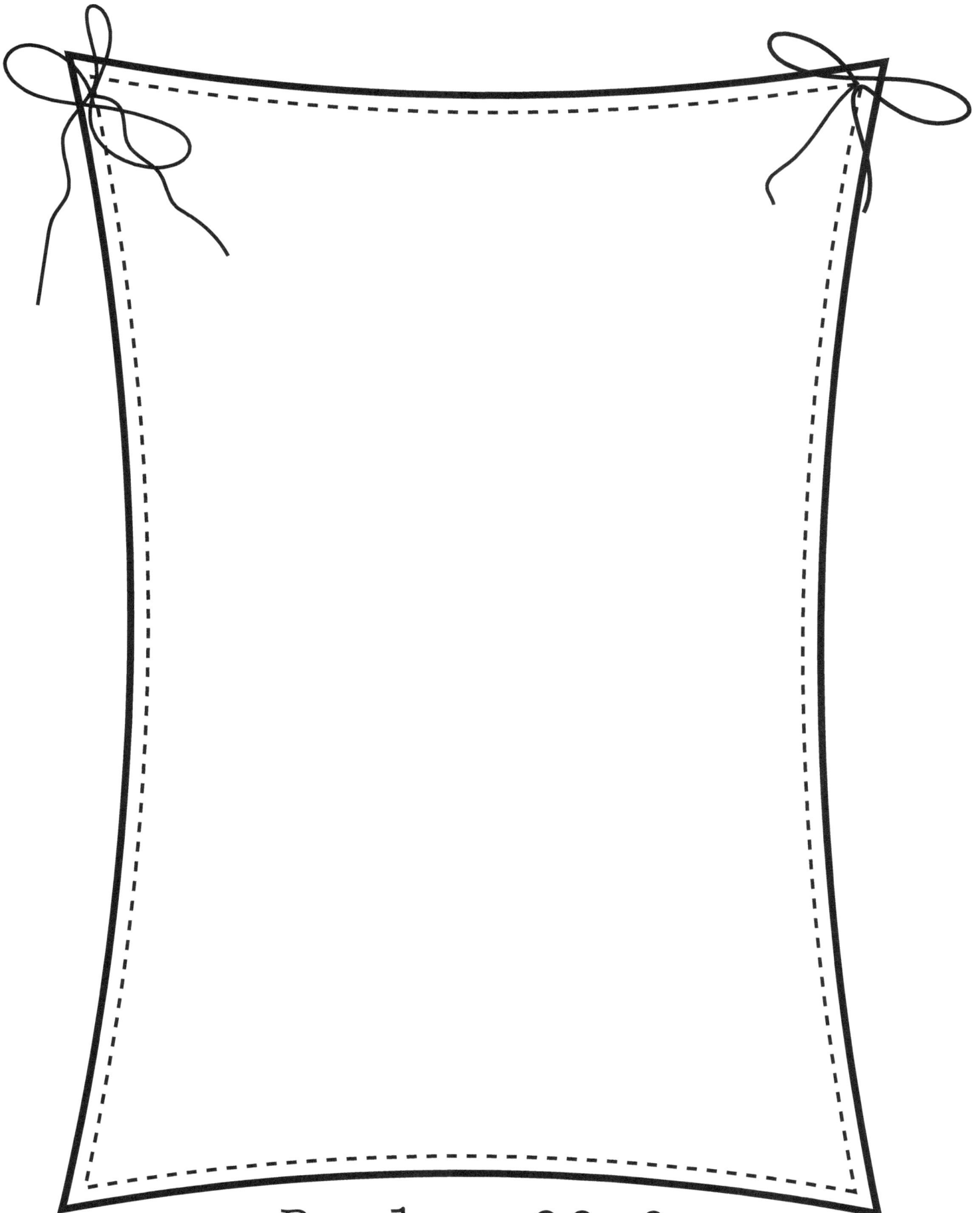

Psalms 22:3

He Inhabits the
Praises
of His People

All of us want to accomplish something important in life. And we devise plans to make that happen. A plan is a detailed strategy for achieving something, with the timing and resources included.

God often gives us a dream or desire, but He doesn't always provide details about the exact time table or the means necessary to fulfill that dream. Does that mean He doesn't care? Quite the contrary.

Entrusting our plans to God brings peace and happiness. By relying on His perfect timing, we have hope and confidence that He is working on our behalf (often behind the scenes) when problems arise.

As you color this page, talk with the Lord about your plans and dreams. Permit Him to direct your steps. Accept His perfect timing.

God won't allow us to succeed at anything, unless we're relying on Him. Humbly trust the Lord to bring success to your plans.

A man's mind plans his way, but the Lord directs his steps and makes them sure. Prov. 16:9

PLANS
PLANS
PLANS

GOD

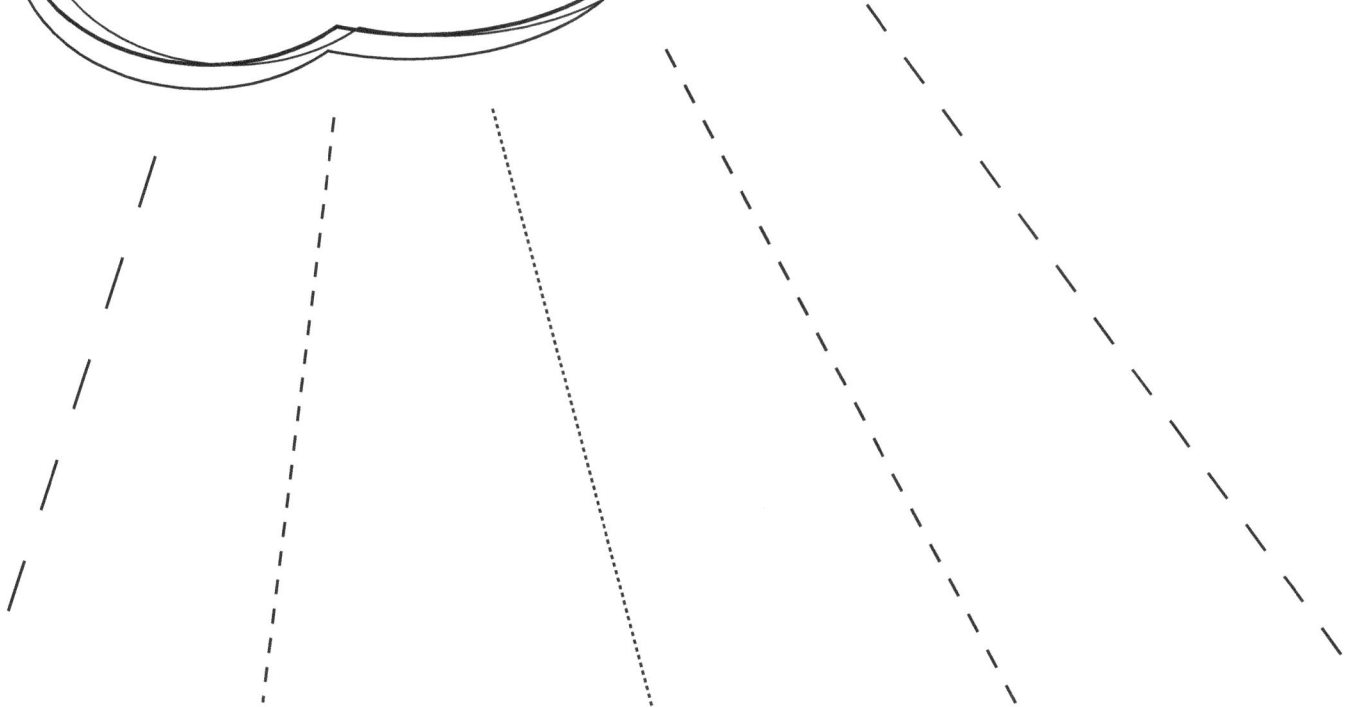

HAS
YOU
COVERED

His Banner Over Me is Love

Be·
You
·tiful

I AM FEARFULLY AND WONDERFULLY MADE IN HIS IMAGE.

We were created to be connected to God, just as the branches of a vine are connected to its stem. As long as we stay connected, His power flows through us.

God is our source. His spiritual energy nourishes and sustains, while we develop and grow.

Our source of life is not within ourselves; it is in Christ and Him alone.

We must stay rightly joined to Him - in relationship with Him - in order to bear fruit. Apart from Christ we can do nothing.

Christians cannot accomplish anything of lasting value without Jesus.

I am the true vine. John 15:1

I am the
VINE,
You are the
BRANCHES

Praises

I will enter His gates with
Thankgiving in my HEART.

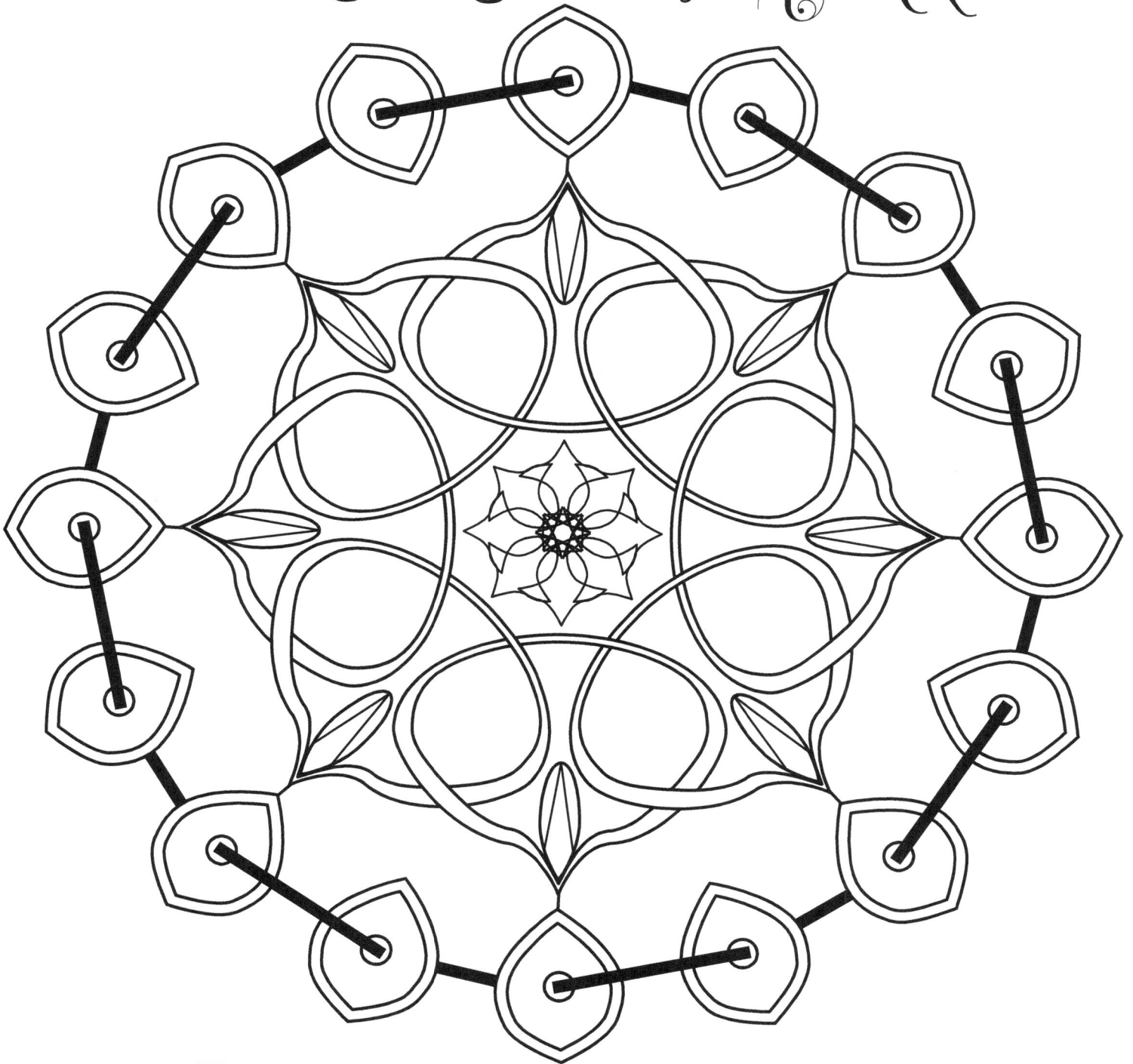

I will enter His courts
with PRAISE.

I will never leave you. I promise.

— God

GOD
IT ALL STARTS WITH GOD

Who has done this
and carried it through,
calling forth the generations
from the beginning?
I, the Lord - with the first of them
and with the last - I am He.
Isaiah 41:4

But those who trust in the Lord will become strong again.
They will be like eagles that grow new feathers.
They will run and not get weak.
They will walk and not get tired.
Isaiah 40:31

Trust the Lord with All Your Heart
Lean Not on Your Own Understanding

In All Your Ways Acknowledge Him
And He Will Make Straight Your Path

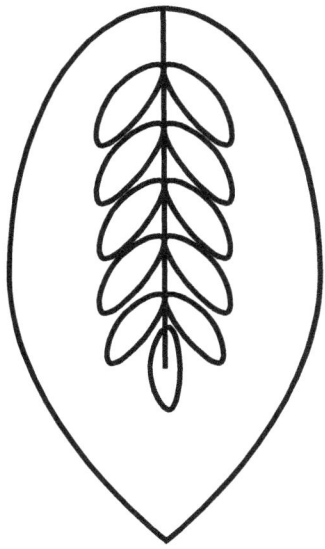

Don't magnify your problems.
Magnify God.

- -
- -
- -
- -
- -
- -
- -
- -
- -
- -
- -

Rejoice in the Lord, always.
Again, I say rejoice.

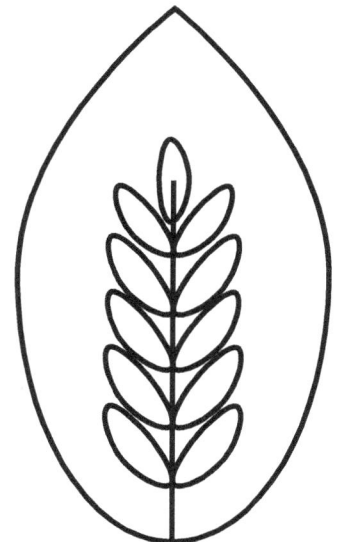

My Soul
Magnifies the
LORD
and My Spirit
Rejoices in
GOD
My Savior.

When asked to list their priorities most Christians say, "God first. Family second. Work last." But if you're like most people, that's easier said, than done! In fact, at times - it's impossible.

Reflect on the challenges you face in putting God first in your life. It may be that you have no problem putting Him first when it comes to prayer and devotion. But, when it comes to trusting God for daily needs, you rely more on your paycheck to provide those necessities.

Or you may go to God when times are hard. But when life is smooth sailing you forget to pray or to be thankful. When do you find it most difficult to keep God as your number one priority?

WHEN WAS THE
LAST
TIME YOU PUT GOD
FIRST?

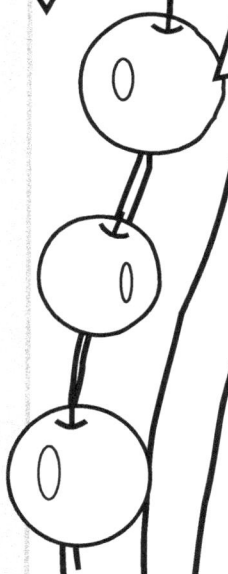

MY HOPES AND DREAMS

It may seem counterintuitive, but you will never fulfill a dream until you're ready to give it up!

Yielding your dreams and desires to God is a part of His process to actually bring them about. God gives us a dream. But He wants us to give it back...in essence, to surrender the details of accomplishing it to His way and within His time.

Ultimately, it builds trust and confidence in our relationship with Him. We can do anything with God's help, including seeing our dreams come to pass.

WHAT DO YOU WANT TO:

DO
SEE
EXPLORE
SHARE
DISCOVER
MAKE
RIDE
VISIT
CREATE
WATCH
GROW
GIVE BACK
BECOME

PRAISE BE TO THE GOD AND FATHER
OF OUR
LORD JESUS CHRIST,
WHO HAS BLESSED US IN
THE HEAVENLY REALMS
WITH EVERY
SPIRITUAL BLESSING IN CHRIST.

SURRENDER

IS EMBRACING

God's Plan

AND LAYING DOWN

Your Own

You are the Lord's celebration.
He delights in you.
You bring a song to His heart.
Today He is singing
His love song over you.

THE LORD YOUR GOD IS WITH YOU.
HE TAKES GREAT DELIGHT IN YOU.
HE REJOICES OVER YOU WITH SINGING.

My Favorite Accomplishments & Achievements Because of the Lord:

THE JOY OF THE LORD IS MY STRENGTH

What are "things" that God never allows to be wasted?

A few are listed to give you a headstart!

– PAIN & SUFFERING

– HURT

– TIME

– WAITING

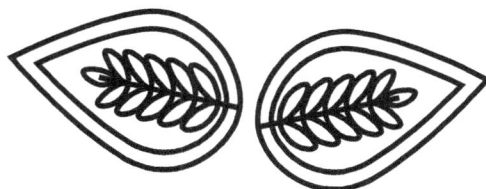

THE
LORD
never
wastes
any
THING

The Lord has hidden himself from His people,

----

but I trust Him and place my hope in Him.

Jesus
Is
Lord

DESCRIBE YOUR FAVORITE TYPE OF MORNING:

The steadfast love of the Lord never ceases;
    His mercies never come to an end.
They are new every morning and great is His faithfulness.

                                    Lamentations 3:22-23

WHY DO WE LOVE GOD?

The Bible confirms that we love, because He first loved us. Love started with God.

He loved us from the beginning, which is the reason we are geared to return that love and to love others.

How will you show God your love today?

Even when we know God's will, we have doubts. Jeremiah, an Old Testament prophet, reminded God of his youth and lack of experience when the Lord commanded him to fight. He was essentially telling God, "I am not sure I can do it!"

But Jeremiah's divine call originated before his birth, even while he was being formed in the womb. And God would be with Jeremiah and provide everything needed to complete that plan.

This same God has a call for you and for me. It really doesn't matter when you came to know Him, because He knew and cared for you in eternity past! What confidence it brings to know that our identity was known by God before we ever spoke a word or made a move.

Rather than doubt your place in this world, trust God and know that you have been chosen for a purpose. That purpose isn't limited by your own weakness, but is achievable by a God who possesses everything you need to make it happen!

Doodle words that describe the gifts and talents God has given you to accomplish His purpose.

YOU
ARE NOT AN ACCIDENT!

I am your creator.
You were in my care before you were born.

www.ingramcontent.com/pod-product-compliance
Lightning Source LLC
Chambersburg PA
CBHW081147040426
42445CB00015B/1791